MAPS and MAPPING

ENVIRONMENTS

By Susan Hoe

Science and curriculum consultant:
Debra Voege, M.A., science curriculum resource teacher

FORD CITY PUBLIC LIBRARY
1136 FOURTH AVENUE
FORD CITY, PA 16226

Gareth Stevens
Publishing

Please visit our web site at www.garethstevens.com
For a free catalog describing our list of high-quality books, call 1-800-542-2595 (USA) or 1-800-387-3178 (Canada).
Our fax: 1-877-542-2596

Library of Congress Cataloging-in-Publication Data available upon request from publisher.

ISBN-10: 0-8368-9204-6   ISBN-13: 978-0-8368-9204-8 (lib. bdg.)
ISBN-10: 0-8368-9331-X   ISBN-13: 978-0-8368-9331-1 (softcover)

This edition first published in 2009 by
Gareth Stevens Publishing
A Weekly Reader® Company
1 Reader's Digest Road
Pleasantville, NY 10570-7000 USA

This U.S. edition copyright © 2009 by Gareth Stevens, Inc. Original edition copyright © 2007 by ticktock Media Ltd. First published in Great Britain in 2008 by ticktock Media Ltd., Unit 2, Orchard Business Centre, North Farm Road, Tunbridge Wells, Kent, TN2 3XF

Gareth Stevens Senior Managing Editor: Lisa M. Herrington
Gareth Stevens Creative Director: Lisa Donovan
Gareth Stevens Art Director: Ken Crossland
Gareth Stevens Associate Editor: Amanda Hudson

Picture credits (t=top; b=bottom; c=center; l=left; r=right):
China Images/Alamy: 17tl; Victor Englebert/photographersdirect.com: 20t, 21t; Getmapping PLC: 24c; Sean Harris: 4b, 8; iStock: 4t, 6t, 7b, 11tr, 11c, 12t, 12b, 19tl, 22t, 25b; Jupiter Images: 2; Lehtikuva Oy/Rex Features: 19tr; Oliver Polet/Corbis: 17b; Ulli Seer/Getty Images: 5t; Shutterstock: 6b, 11tl, 11b, 15bl, 15br, 17tr, 18b, 19b, 24tl, 24b, 25t, 25c; Justin Spain: 4c, 9 all, 21b, 31t; Hayley Terry: 5b, 10, 13 all, 15t, 19c, 27, 30; Tim Thirlaway: 28, 29; Time and Life Pictures/Getty Images: 20b; www.mapart.co.uk: 7t, 14, 16, 18, 22b, 23, 26, 31b.

Every effort has been made to trace the copyright holders for the photos used in this book, and the publisher apologizes in advance for any unintentional omissions. We would be pleased to insert the appropriate acknowledgments in any subsequent edition of this publication.

All rights reserved. No part of this book may be reproduced, stored in a retrieval system, or transmitted in any form or by any means, electronic, mechanical, photocopying, recording, or otherwise, without the prior written permission of the copyright holder.

Printed in the United States of America

1 2 3 4 5 6 7 8 9 10 09 08

Contents

What Is a Map? 4

Why Do We Need Maps? 6

Mapping Your Classroom 8

Mapping a Place for a New School 10

Planning Changes in a Town 12

Roads Across Your Country 14

Mapping Where People Live Around the World 16

View of a Rain Forest 18

Mapping a Rain Forest Village 20

Measuring for Maps 22

Mapping With Computers 24

Acts of Nature and Weather Events 26

Mapping a Beach of Your Own 28

Glossary 30

Index 32

Words in **bold** are defined in the glossary.

What Is a Map?

A **map** is a special drawing. This kind of drawing shows parts of an area. The area is drawn as if seen from above.

A map can show an area as big as the world. Or it can be as small as a classroom in your school!

4

Making a Map of an Island

Map Key

- Trees/woods
- Roads/footpaths
- Gray-roofed building
- Red-roofed building
- Pier
- Gardens

Maps help us see things as if we were directly above them.

In this book, we will learn how maps tell us about the **environment**. But first let's look at some of the ways that maps help us.

Find the piers on the map. Find the longest one.

Now look for the longest pier in the photo.

5

Why Do We Need Maps?

Maps help us find our way around. They give us all kinds of information about where we live.

A map can help you get from one place to another. It can show you where you are. It can show where to go and how to get there.

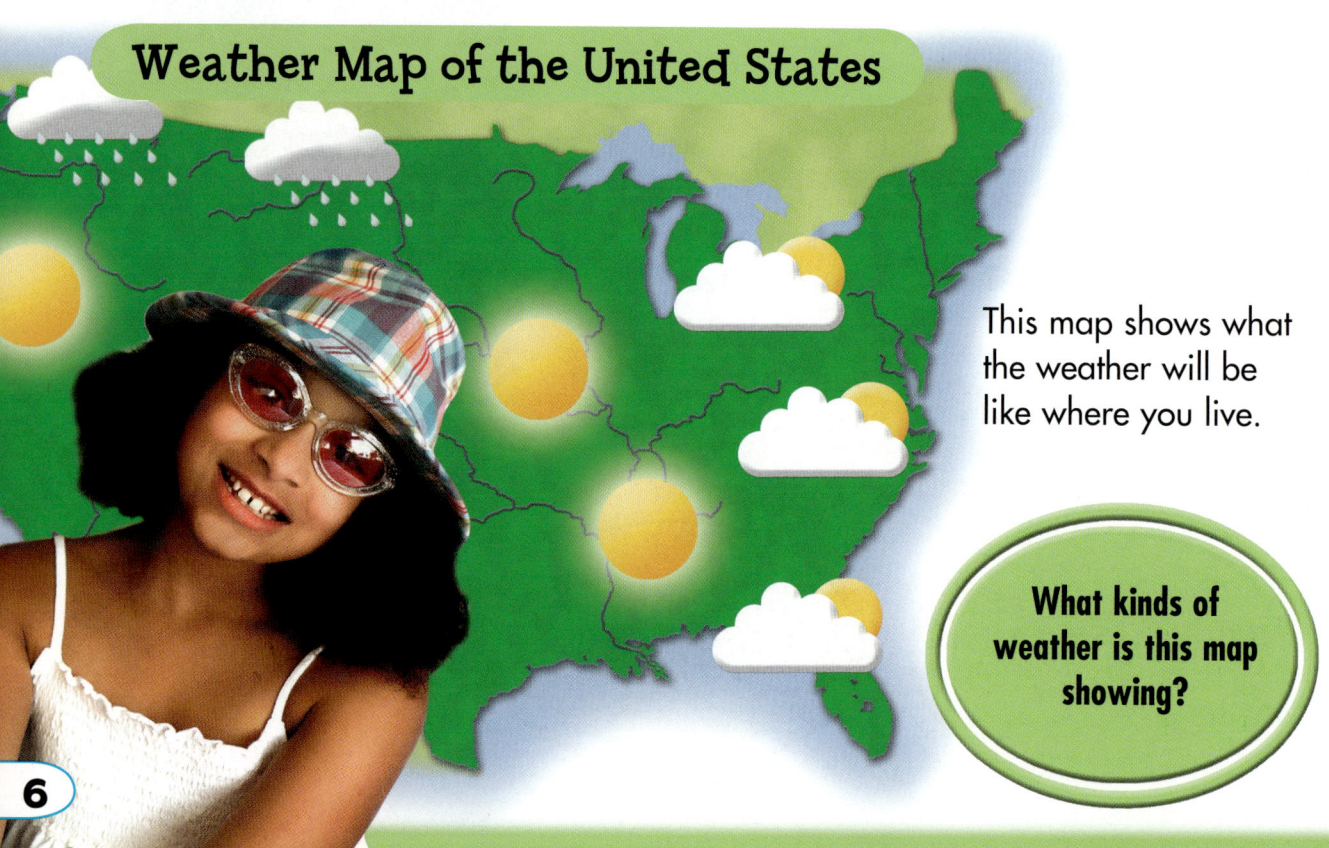

Weather Map of the United States

This map shows what the weather will be like where you live.

What kinds of weather is this map showing?

6

Map of the World

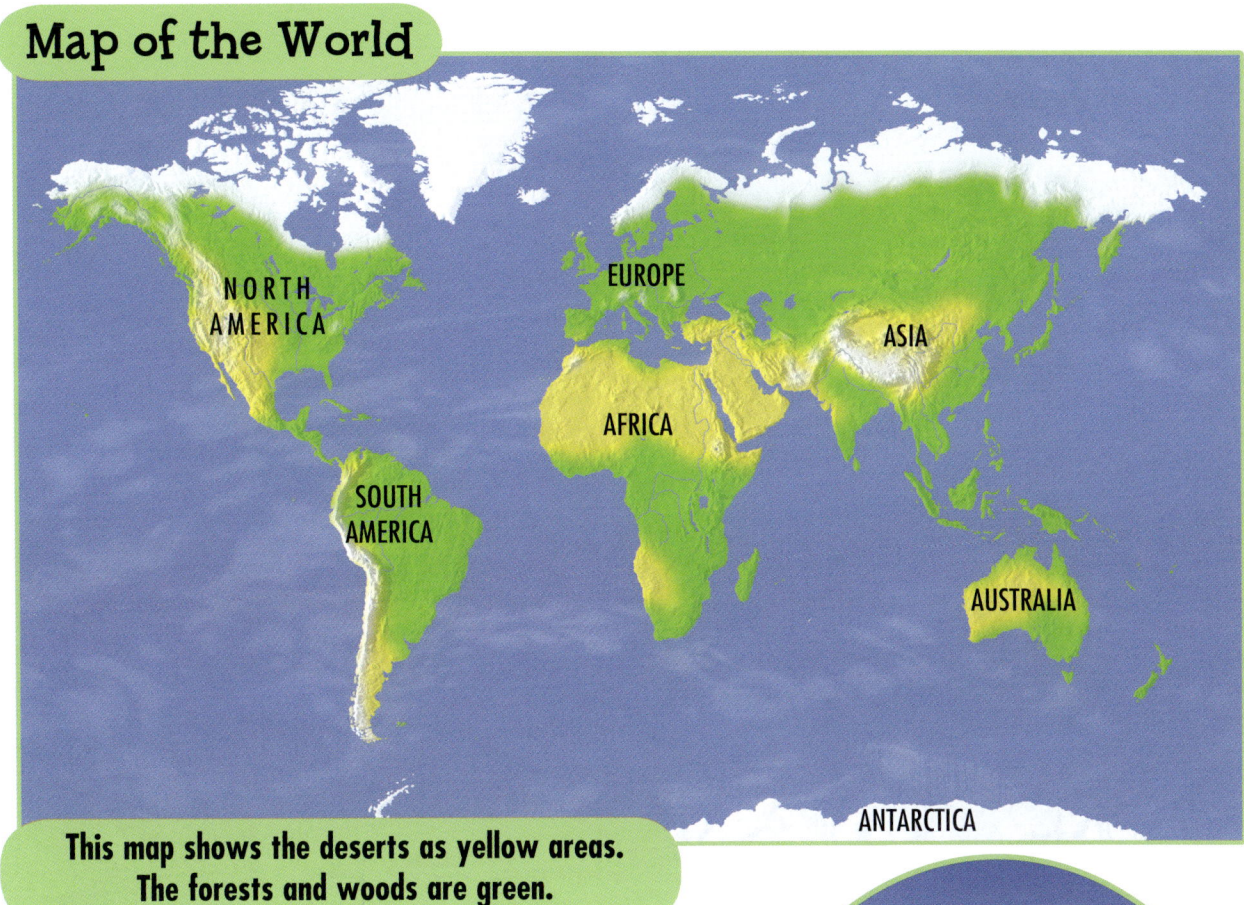

This map shows the deserts as yellow areas. The forests and woods are green.

Maps teach us important facts about places. We can learn about places close to home or on the other side of the world.

Maps can show whether land is flat or has hills. They can show where people and animals live. We can also learn what crops are grown. We can see what sorts of things are made in a place.

Maps are handy and easy to use. They can show us huge areas in a small amount of space. We can take them just about anywhere!

Mapping Your Classroom

Maps show a place as if you were looking down on it. That place can be your country or your town. It can even be a classroom in your school!

A 3-D classroom

This classroom is a **three-dimensional (3-D)** space. The room and things in the room are solid. They have length, width, and **depth**.

A 2-D Map

A map is a **two-dimensional (2-D)** drawing of a space. Everything on the map of the classroom looks flat.

To create a map, all the flat shapes are drawn on a piece of paper.

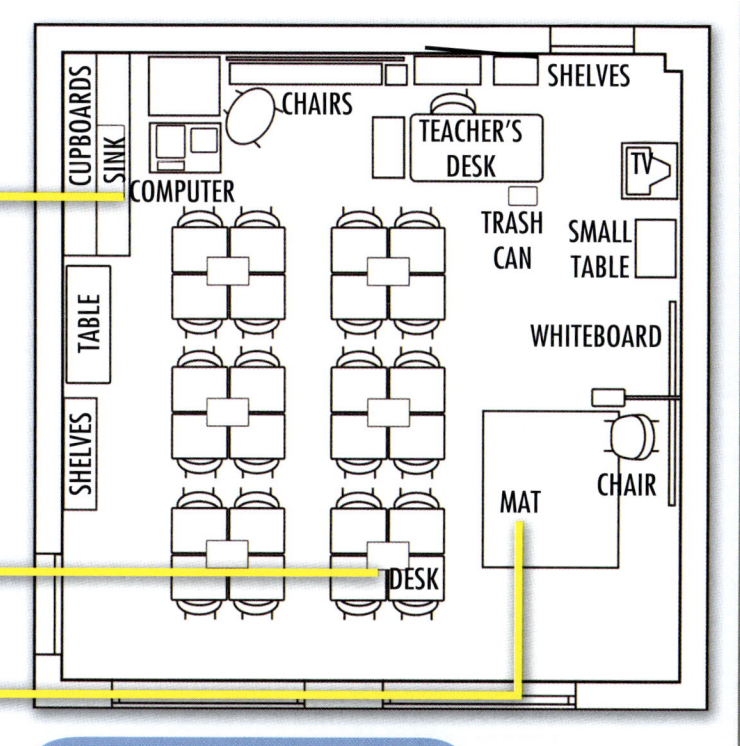

A 2–D map of a 3–D classroom

This map shows you how to find everything in the classroom.

- Find the teacher's desk.
- Find the shelves.

Making the Map

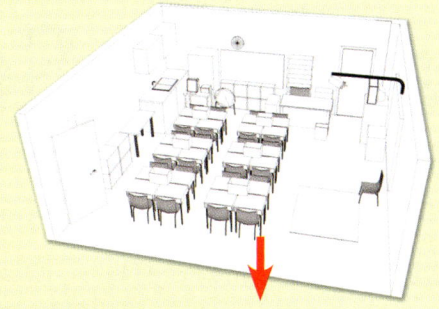

This drawing of the classroom was made from photos.

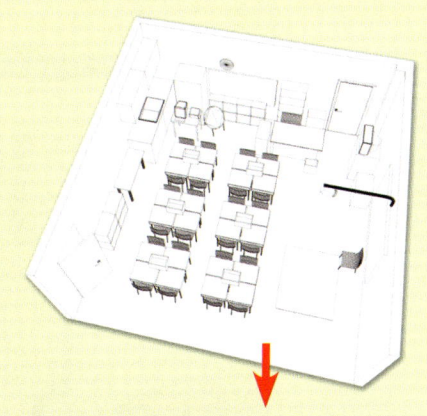

Pretend you are able to float up above the room. Imagine looking down on it.

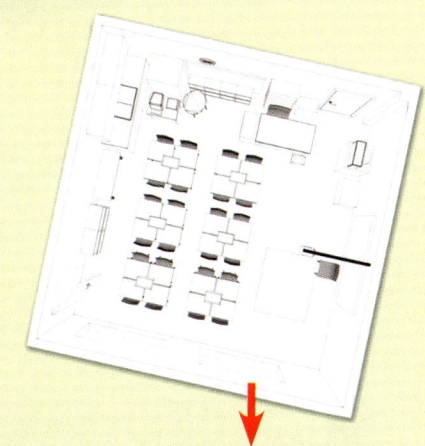

When you are right above the room, it looks flat. This is the view used to make a 2-D map.

9

Mapping a Place for a New School

A new school needs lots of land. It needs room for a school building. There must be space for a parking lot and a playground. The school needs special **services** from the town.

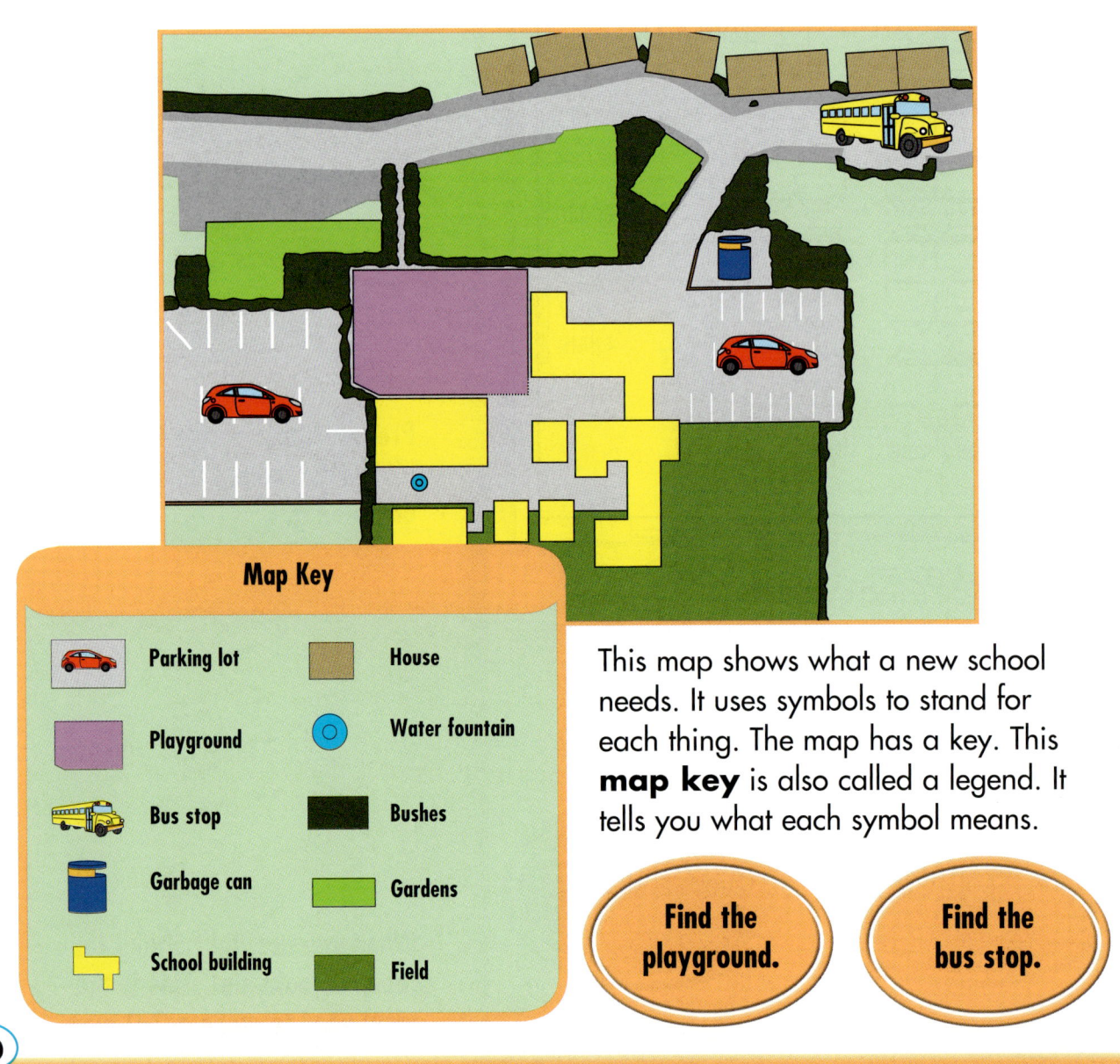

Map Key

- 🚗 Parking lot
- 🟪 Playground
- 🚌 Bus stop
- 🗑 Garbage can
- 🟨 School building
- ⬜ House
- 🔵 Water fountain
- ⬛ Bushes
- 🟩 Gardens
- 🟢 Field

This map shows what a new school needs. It uses symbols to stand for each thing. The map has a key. This **map key** is also called a legend. It tells you what each symbol means.

Find the playground.

Find the bus stop.

Town Services

Towns provide many services that schools need.

The electrical plant supplies electricity to the school.

Some towns have **reservoirs**. They hold the water used by homes, buses, businesses, and schools. This reservoir (above) is formed by a large **dam**.

New roads are built so that students can get to school.

Some of the school's garbage may be taken to a dump. Other items are taken to a **recycling** plant.

Planning Changes in a Town

When a new building goes up, it causes changes in the area.

A new school can mean more classrooms and better equipment.

A new building can cause extra traffic. More traffic can mean more air **pollution** from cars. People who build new buildings must plan for that.

Making Good Choices When Planning

The town of Mapleville needs a new hospital. You must decide where to build it. Look at this map of Mapleville and the two hospital plans. Which plan would you choose? Which one would be better for the town's environment? Which would harm fewer fields, forests, and lakes? Why?

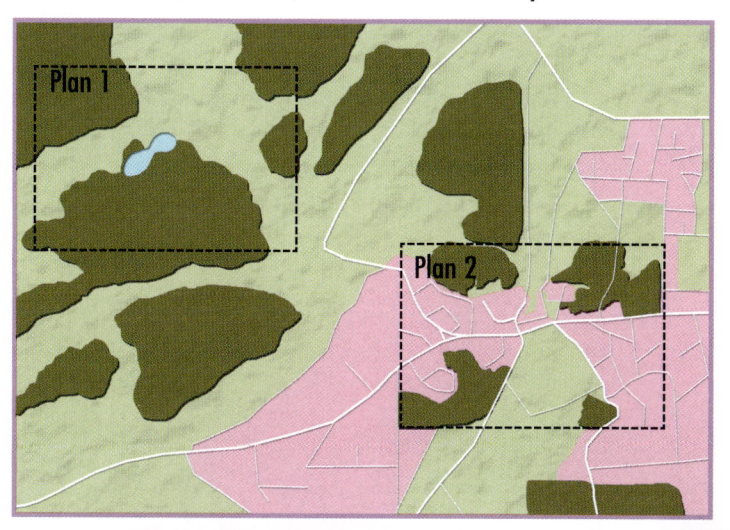

Map Key

- Field
- Forest
- Lake
- Road
- Town
- Proposed site

Plan 1

The hospital will be built in a wooded area far from town. There are no roads around. Trees must be cut down. The pond must be emptied and filled with dirt to make more land. A road and parking lot will be built.

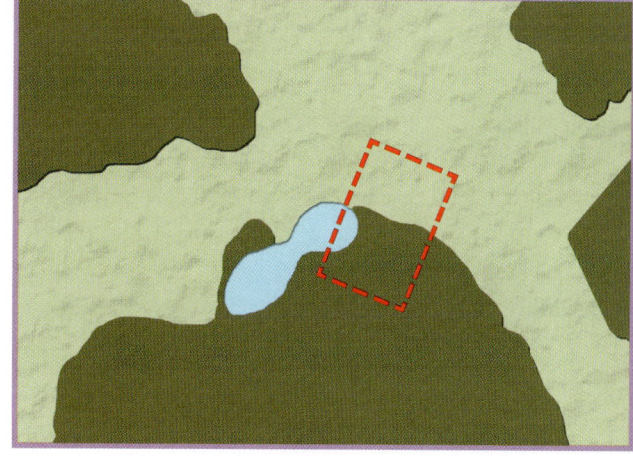

Plan 2

The hospital will be built in a field that is near a main road. More trees will be planted around the building. A parking lot will be built under the ground. It will not be seen from the road.

Roads Across Your Country

You can show more than just the streets of a town on a map. You can show the roads of a whole country! Highways help people move **goods** across the United States.

This map shows the major roads in the United States. Roads that connect states are called interstate highways. They go through cities, mountains, coastal areas, deserts, and waterways. Some go east and west. Some go north and south. Many cross over each other.

The **compass rose** on this map shows you which direction is north (N), south (S), east (E), or west (W). It also shows northeast (NE), southeast (SE), southwest (SW), and northwest (NW).

Roads, bridges, airports, and railroads connect different areas of the United States.

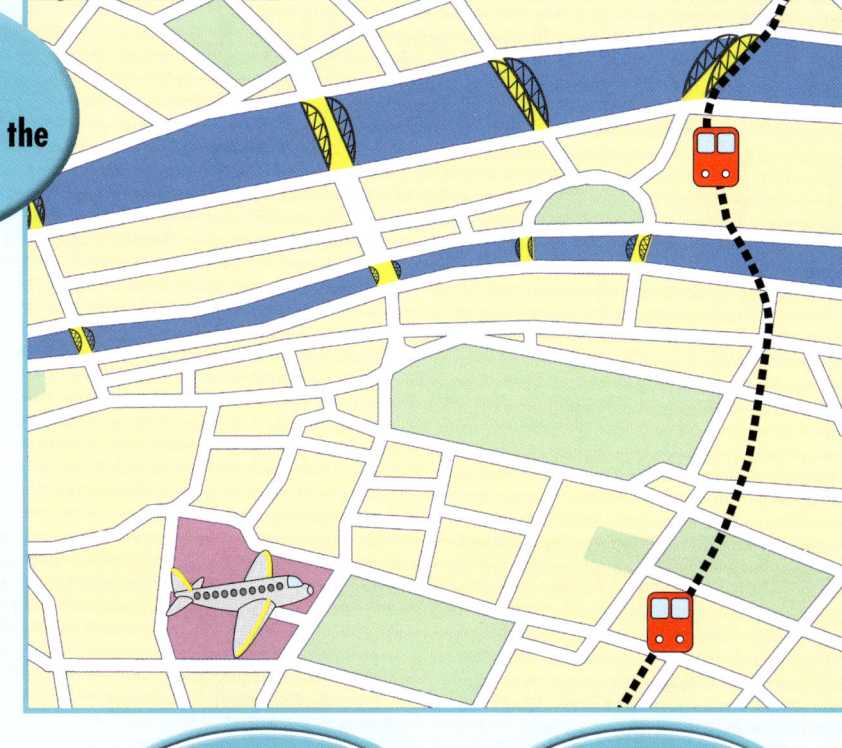

Map Key

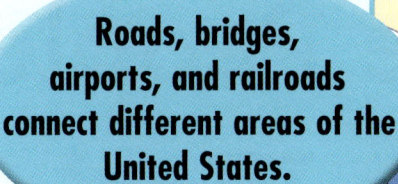

- Bridge
- Railroad track
- Airport
- Road
- River
- Grassland

This city map shows roads and other **structures**.

Find a bridge.

Find the railroad track.

On the Road

Be kind to the environment when traveling by car.

Keep roads and highways clean. Help protect the natural beauty of the area.

Travel with bags to store your trash. Empty them into garbage cans.

15

Mapping Where People Live Around the World

Most people live where there is water and food. They also want safe roads to get from place to place. Finding a good job is important in where to live, too.

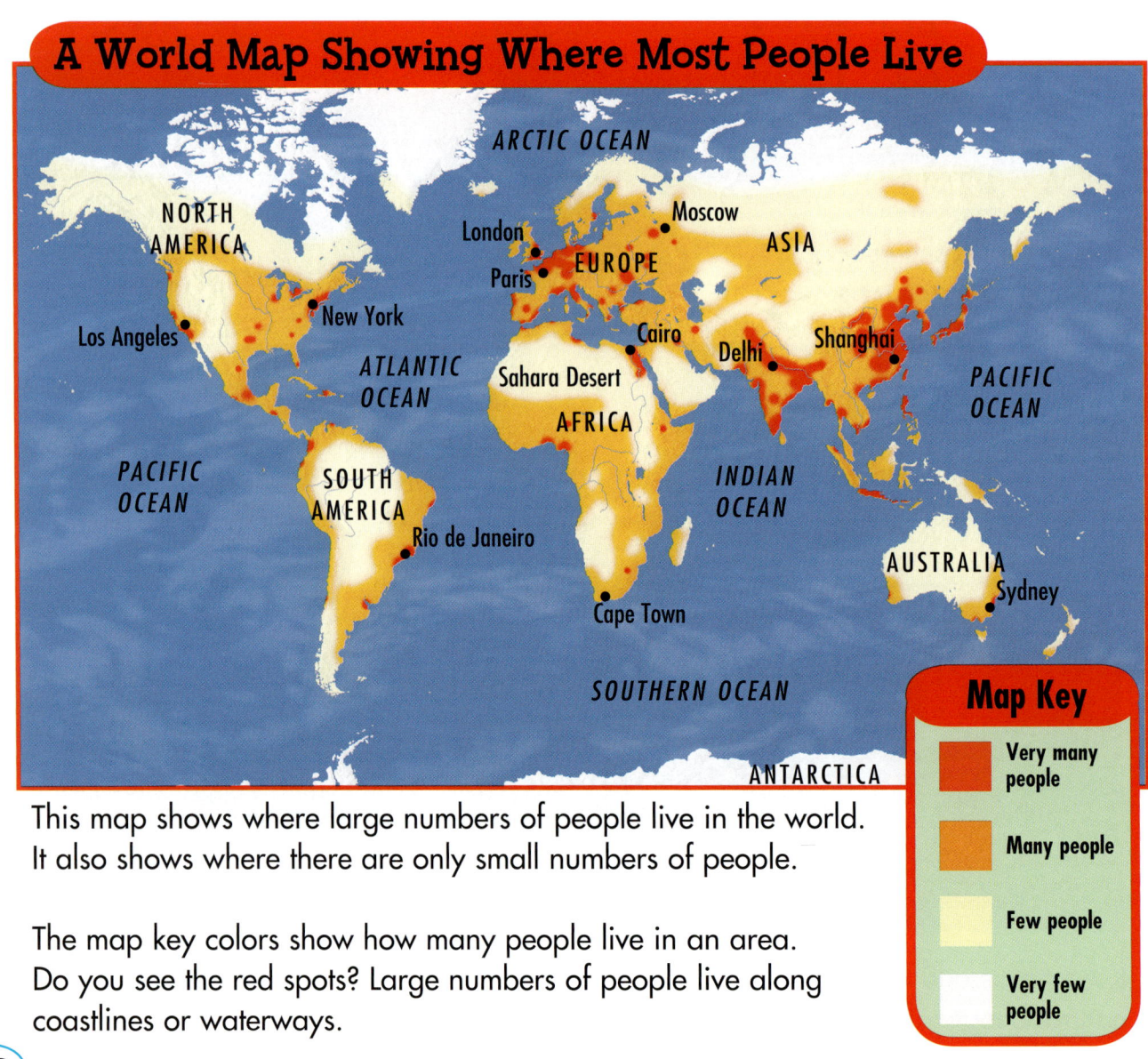

A World Map Showing Where Most People Live

Map Key
- Very many people
- Many people
- Few people
- Very few people

This map shows where large numbers of people live in the world. It also shows where there are only small numbers of people.

The map key colors show how many people live in an area. Do you see the red spots? Large numbers of people live along coastlines or waterways.

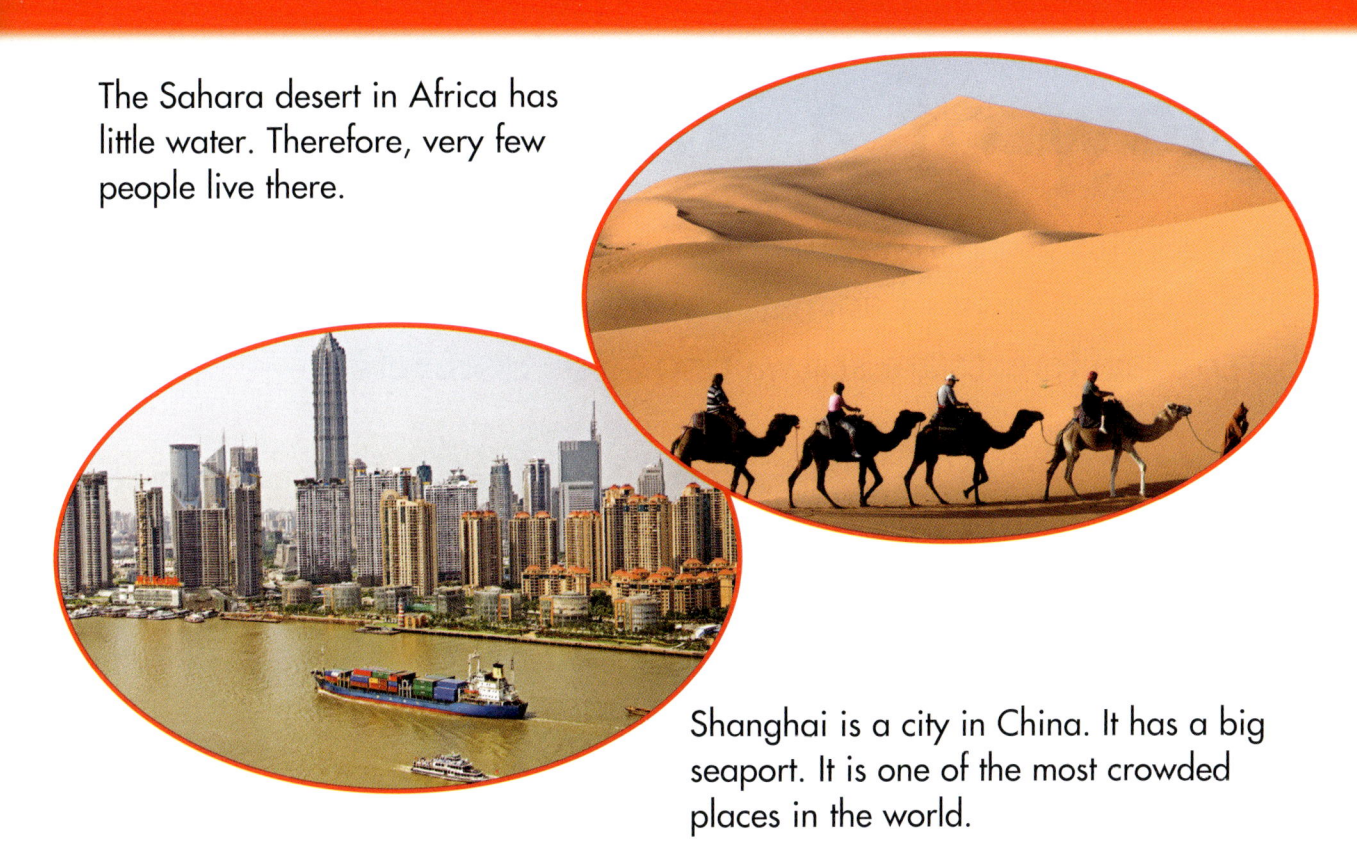

The Sahara desert in Africa has little water. Therefore, very few people live there.

Shanghai is a city in China. It has a big seaport. It is one of the most crowded places in the world.

Fighting Pollution

People are the cause of most pollution in the world. But people also help fix many pollution problems. **Governments** and **aid agencies** are working to clean up the environment.

The new well in this African village has been built to help people.

View of a Rain Forest

Rain forests are lush, warm areas with heavy rainfall. Many plants grow there. Millions of animals live there, too. Some living things in Earth's rain forests are still waiting to be discovered!

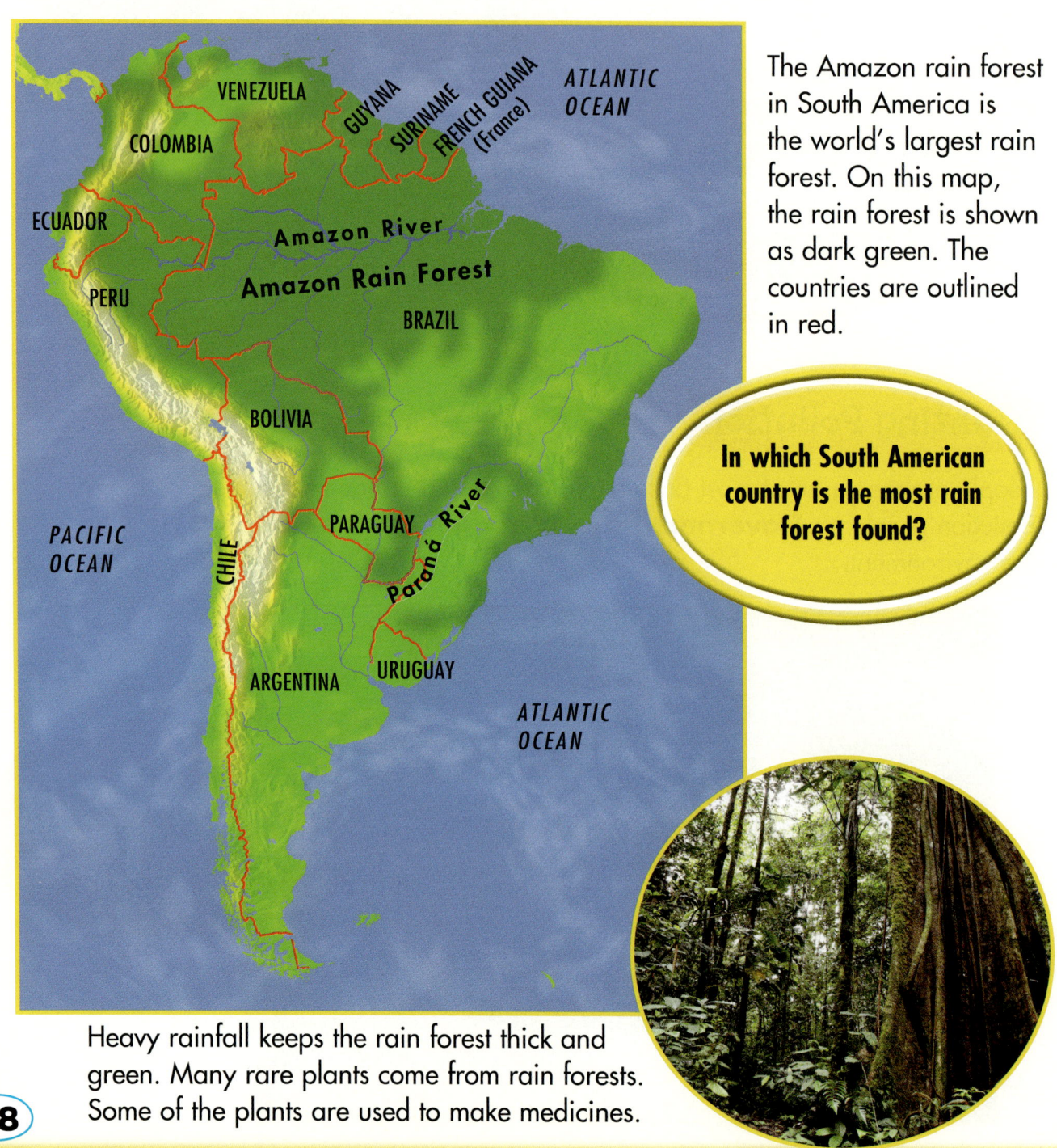

The Amazon rain forest in South America is the world's largest rain forest. On this map, the rain forest is shown as dark green. The countries are outlined in red.

In which South American country is the most rain forest found?

Heavy rainfall keeps the rain forest thick and green. Many rare plants come from rain forests. Some of the plants are used to make medicines.

The rain forests are getting smaller. Too many trees are being cut down. This is called "deforestation."

The harpy eagle is in danger of becoming **extinct.**

When trees are cut down, many animals lose their homes. Some of the animals die out.

Deforestation of a Rain Forest

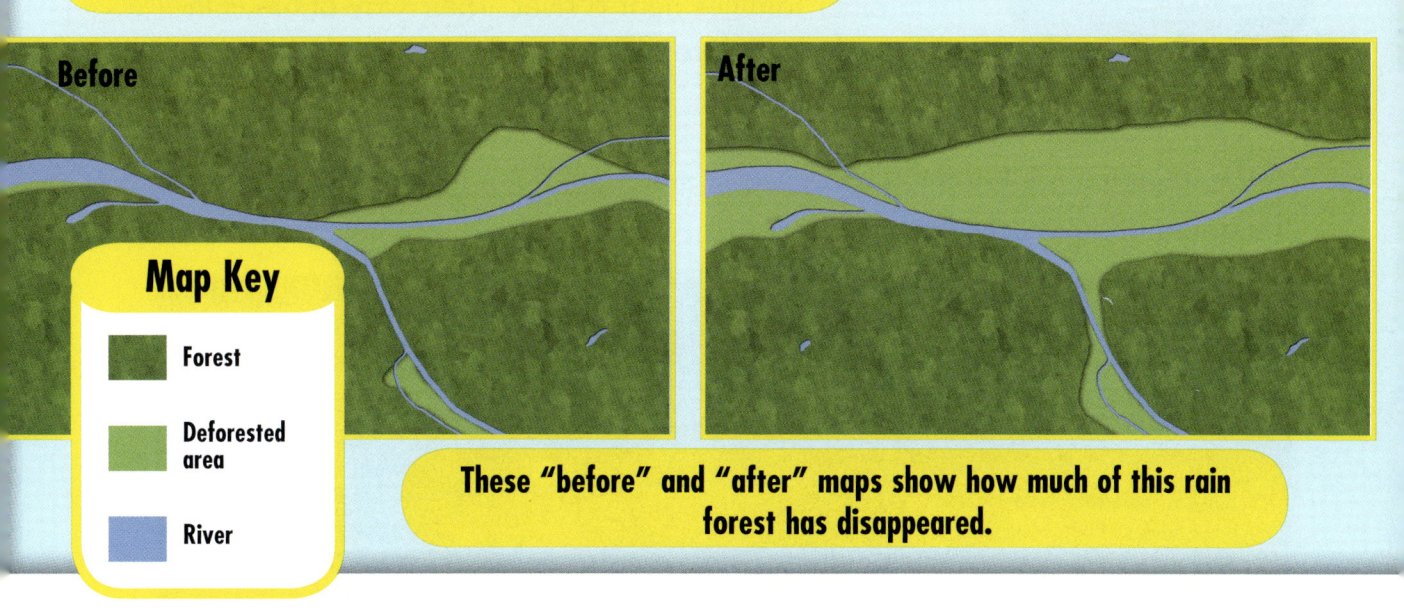

Before

After

Map Key
- Forest
- Deforested area
- River

These "before" and "after" maps show how much of this rain forest has disappeared.

How Can You Help?

Paper is made from wood. Try to recycle paper. That way, fewer trees are cut down to make new paper. When you buy paper, look for the symbol on the right. It means the paper is recycled.

People work to save rain forests and the animals that live there.

Mapping a Rain Forest Village

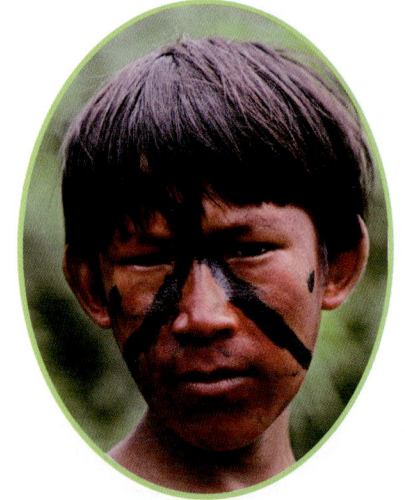

The rain forests of Brazil are home to different groups of people. One group is the Yanomami.

This is Shoco, a young Yanomami boy. His family lives with other families near a river. Their way of life is in danger from deforestation.

The Yanomami eat fish that they catch in the river. They also eat meat from the animals they hunt in the rain forest.

Shoco and his family sleep in hammocks that are hung inside their house.

Shoco's Home

The group gathers nuts and fruits in the rain forest. They also grow sweet potatoes and plantains (a type of banana) in their gardens.

The map below shows Shoco's home. The map symbols stand for different parts of the house. The map key helps you understand what the symbols mean.

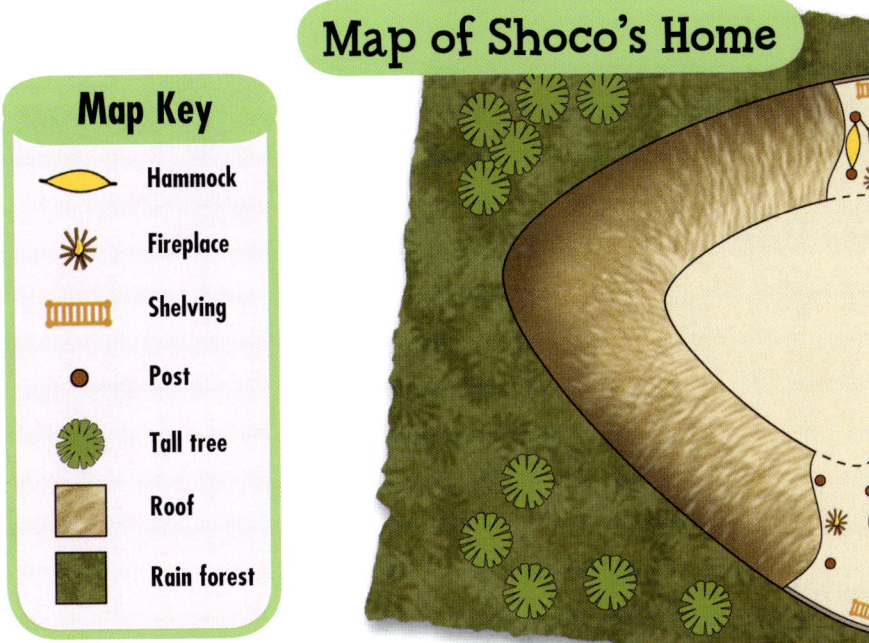

The Yanomami live together in a large house. It is shaped like a doughnut and called a shabono.

Map of Shoco's Home

Map Key

- Hammock
- Fireplace
- Shelving
- Post
- Tall tree
- Roof
- Rain forest

21

Measuring for Maps

Before you can draw a map, you must figure out the size and shape of the area. This means figuring out how to measure large areas.

> This man uses special equipment to measure distances between points.

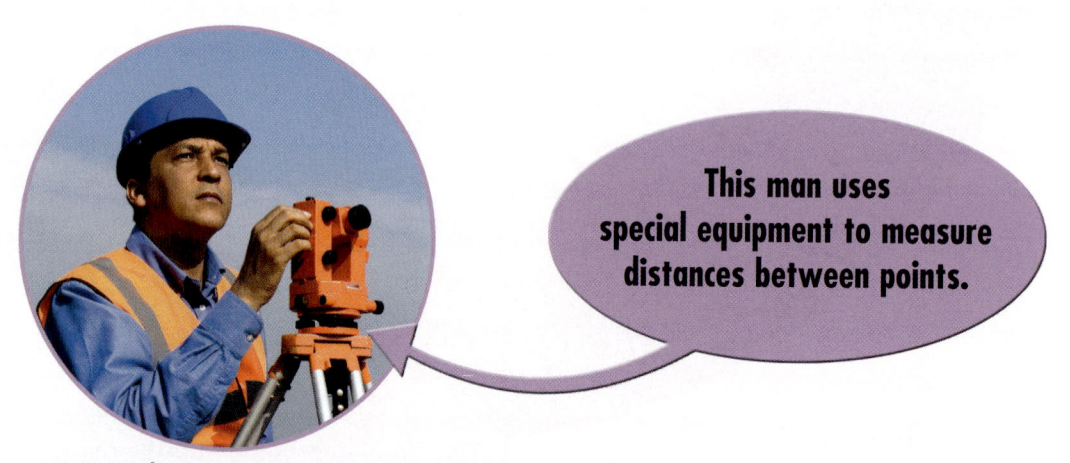

Mapmakers use their measurements to draw their maps. The maps on these pages show an amusement park.

Scale: Shrinking to Fit

Mapmakers gather all their measurements. Then they figure out how to fit them onto a piece of paper. So they shrink, or **scale** down, the real measurements to make a map.

This map shows a fairly large area. It uses a scale of 50 feet (15 meters). Many objects can be seen, but they are quite small.

Different scales can be used to map the same area. A different scale can change what you see. Some maps show large areas on a sheet of paper. Other maps show smaller areas, so the same objects look bigger and have more features.

> The map scale is like a ruler. It shows the connection between distance on the map and distance on the ground. This way you can figure out real distances on the map.

0 — 25 feet

This map shows a smaller area than the first map. This map uses a scale of 25 feet (8 m). You see fewer objects on this map, but they seem closer.

0 — 15 feet

This map has the largest scale. It shows an even smaller area. You see fewer objects, but they seem even closer.

23

Mapping With Computers

Many years ago, people had to travel to figure out the shape of the land. Today, mapmakers use computer equipment.

Mapmakers can take many photographs of the ground from an airplane.

This photograph shows the ground as seen from the airplane.

Pictures and measurements are taken from an airplane and sent to computers. The computers use the pictures to draw maps.

Satellites also take pictures of Earth from space.

A satellite circling Earth

Pictures are taken from space, too. The pictures are sent back to Earth. They are put together to make full pictures of our planet, like the one shown here. These pictures can then be turned into maps.

Changing Maps

Satellites can produce road maps that help you find your way. These maps change as you move. The maps are called GPS, or Global Positioning System, maps.

A GPS map at work in a car

25

Acts of Nature and Weather Events

Sudden events such as earthquakes or hurricanes can cause great harm to a place.

- Volcanic Eruption 1985
- Hurricane 1988, 2004
- Hurricane 1996
- Earthquake 1949
- Earthquake 1970
- Wildfire 1998
- Earthquake 2007
- Tsunami 1868
- Hurricane 2004
- Earthquake 1939
- Tornado 1973
- Earthquake 1944

South America has had many natural disasters. Here's a way to map out these events from the past.

Making a Map of Natural Disasters

1. Copy the map of South America on page 26 onto a blank sheet of paper. You could also use thin paper to trace the map.

2. Now make a map key. Draw the symbols below. Show earthquakes, volcanic eruptions, tsunamis, hurricanes, tornadoes, and wildfires.

3. The map on page 26 shows where these storms and other events happened. Draw symbols of these events on your map of South America. Be sure to use symbols that look like the ones in your map key.

Map Key

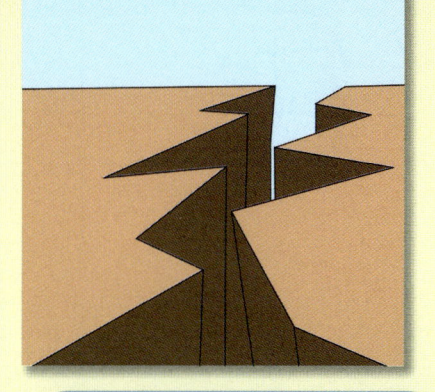

Earthquake: a strong shaking of the ground

Volcanic eruption: when hot rock from inside the earth bursts out of a volcano

Tsunami (tidal wave): a giant wave caused by an earthquake under the ocean

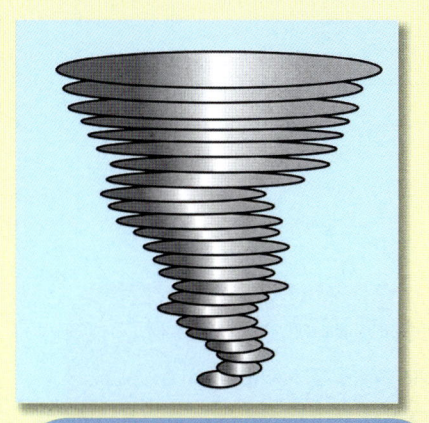

Tornado: wind shaped like a funnel, which can throw heavy objects

Wildfire: a very bad fire that spreads quickly through forest areas

Hurricane: a strong storm with high winds and heavy rains

Mapping a Beach of Your Own

A beach is a fun place to visit. Why not make your own beach map? Make a map key, too, so your friends can find all the great things at your beach.

What kind of shape will your beach have?

How many lifeguard stations will it have? Where will they be placed?

Alex's Amazing Beach

What fun things can people do at your beach? Will there be a pier for fishing? Will there be boats, a snack stand, or a mini golf course?

Does your beach have restrooms? Does it have outdoor showers, a parking lot, or a first-aid station?

28

Step 1

Draw the shape of your beach on a piece of paper. Is it on an ocean or a lake?

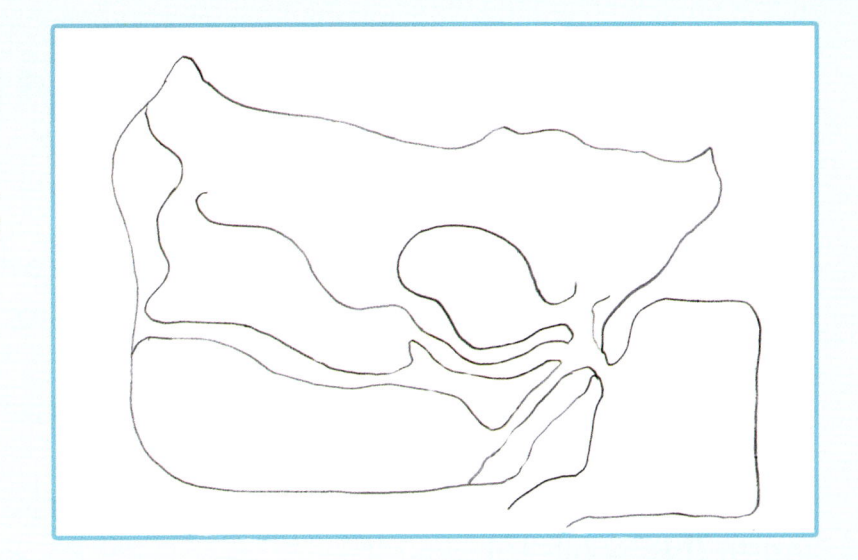

Step 2

Make up symbols for all the items you want to include on your map. Be sure you leave enough space between the symbols. Draw in the sandy beach area. Show grassy areas and parking lots.

Step 3

Color your beach map, and give the beach a name.

Step 4

Make your map key using the symbols on your map.

Map Key

- Water
- Shower
- Snack stand
- Mini golf
- Pier
- Sand
- Restrooms
- Parking
- Lifeguard station
- Water fountain
- First aid
- Rowboats for hire
- Grass
- Trash can
- Picnic area
- Play area

29

Glossary

aid agencies: groups that help people who are poor or who have been affected by wars or disasters

compass rose: a drawing that shows directions on a map — north (N), south (S), east (E) and west (W)

dam: a wall that holds back water

depth: the length from the top of a space or an object to the bottom

environment: the area and space where people, plants, and animals live

equipment: tools and other items used for a job

extinct: having died out

goods: items that people grow or make. People buy and sell goods.

governments: the groups of people who make the laws and rule in a country or an area

map: a picture or chart showing features of an area

map key: the space on a map that shows the meaning of any pictures or colors used on the map

pollution: unclean things found in the air, soil, or water

rain forests: large wooded areas with lots of warm rainfall that produce big trees and shrubs. Little sunlight gets through the thick growths of trees.

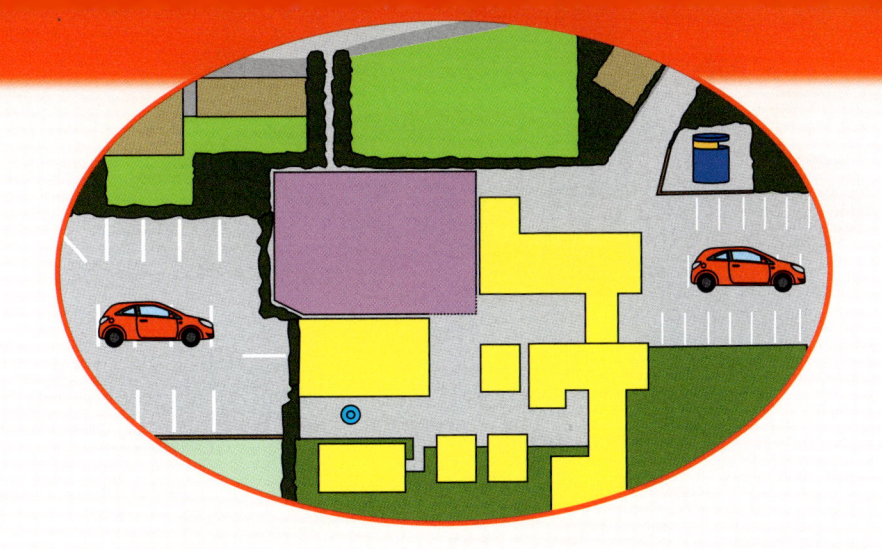

recycling: turning garbage into something that can be used again — especially cans, glass, plastic, and paper

reservoirs: places where fresh water is collected and stored for people to use

scale: the amount by which the measurement of an area is shrunk to fit a map. The scale is a drawing or symbol that tells how to measure distances on the map.

services: needed help offered to people living in an area. Some services are garbage disposal, recycling, water, and electricity.

structures: buildings and other large objects made by people

three-dimensional (3-D): appearing as a solid thing that has length, width, and depth

two-dimensional (2-D): appearing as a flat shape with only length and width

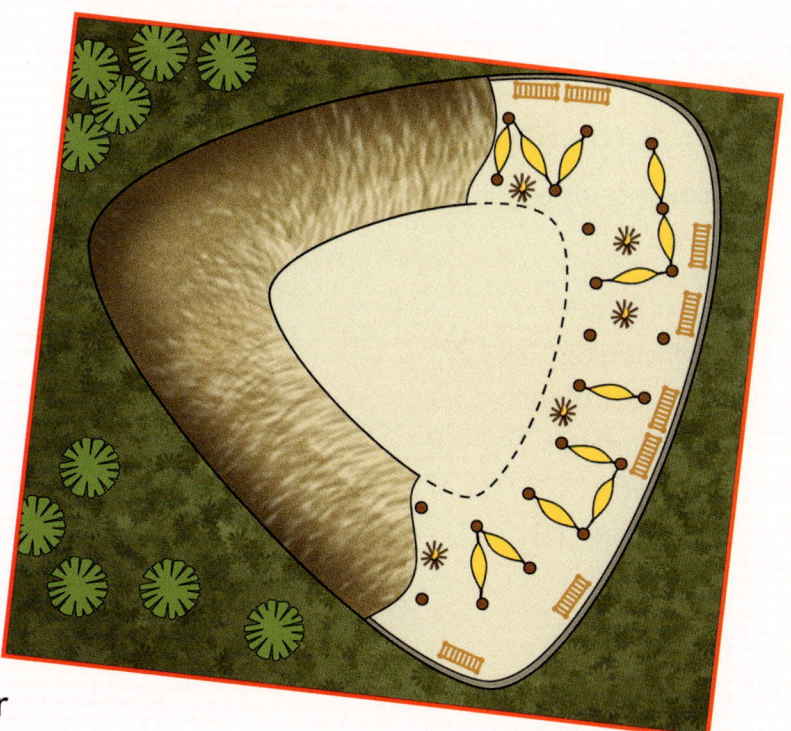

Index

A
Africa 17
aid agencies 17
airplanes 24
amusement parks 22–23

B
beaches 28–29
Brazil 20–21

C
China 17
classrooms 4, 8–9
compass roses 14
computers 24
crops 7

D
deforestation 19, 20
drawing maps 22–29
dump 11

E
earthquakes 26, 27
electrical plants 11
environments 12–13, 14–15
extinction 19

G
garbage 11
goods 14
GPS 25

H
hammocks 20, 21
Harpy eagles 19
hospitals 13
hurricanes 26, 27

I
Interstate highways 14
islands 5

M
map keys 5, 10, 13, 15, 16, 19, 21, 27, 29
mapmaking 9, 22–23, 24–25
measuring areas 22
medicines 18

P
people, mapping where they live 16–17
photographs 9, 24, 25
pollution 12, 17

R
rain forests 18–19, 20–21
recycling 11, 19
reservoirs 11
roads 11, 13–14, 15, 25

S
Sahara desert 17
satellites 25
scale 22–23
schools 8, 10–11, 12
services 10–11
Shabonos 21
Shanghai 17
South America 18–21, 26-27
symbols 10, 19, 21, 27, 29

T
tornadoes 26–27
towns 10–11, 12–13
tsunamis 26–27

U
United States 6, 14–15

V
village 20–21
volcanic eruptions 26–27

W
wells 17
wildfires 26–27
world maps 7, 16

Y
Yanomami 20–21